WHEN YOU LOVE A CAT

WRITTEN BY **M.H. Clark**

ILLUSTRATED & DESIGNED BY **Jessica Phoenix**

When you love a cat, you are chosen, over and over again, each day, for a lifetime.

The space on your lap is taken.
And the space in your heart is, too.

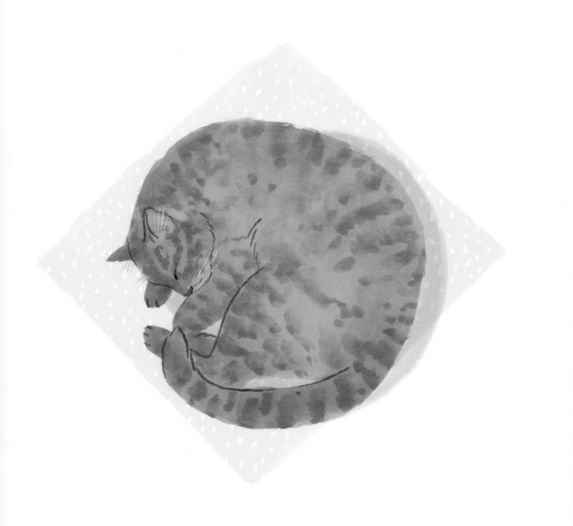

And the daily routines are silly and simple and beautiful,

and somehow, each small moment grows bigger.

So the days come to
mean much more.

When you love a cat, you are wanted—for a snuggle in the night, and on long afternoons.

And there's a favorite shadow

that follows you from room to room.

When you love a cat, you speak
a language of little sounds and gestures.

(It's a secret language, but you
both know what it means.)

You don't need to say a word.
You are already known.

And it is always good—
so good—that you are home.

When you love a cat, the moment
worth living is this one. Right here,
in this window, and this patch of sun.

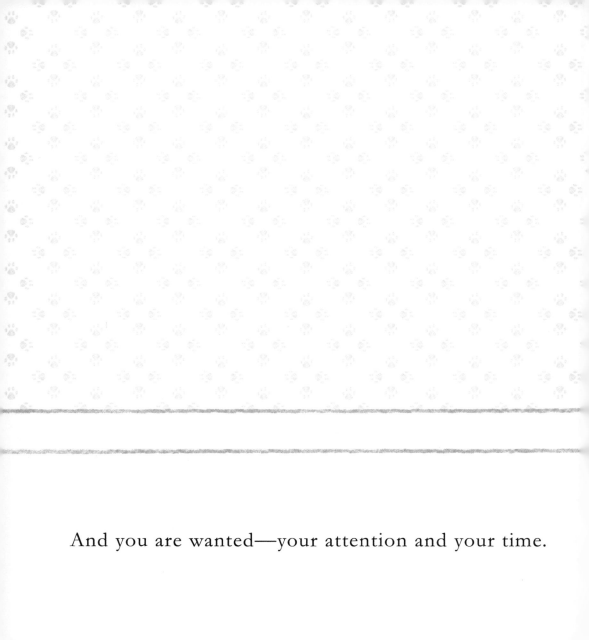

And you are wanted—your attention and your time.

And a happy head bumps up
against you, to say: *you're mine.*

And there is time to play,

and time to share, and time to be spent.

And time to not do anything,
except just be content.

When you love a cat, you share
it all—the gray days and the light.

And that's more than enough.
It's everything—to have
something so simple and right.

When you love a cat, you've been chosen.
And you know it was meant to be—

it's a gift beyond imagining—
this being has chosen me.

COMPENDIUM®
live inspired

Written by: M.H. Clark
Illustrated & Designed by: Jessica Phoenix
Edited by: Kristin Eade
Art Direction by: Megan Gandt Guansing

Library of Congress Control Number: 2017957917 | ISBN: 978-1-943200-99-3

6th printing. Printed in China with soy inks on FSC®-Mix certified paper.

Create meaningful moments with gifts that inspire.

CONNECT WITH US
live-inspired.com | sayhello@compendiuminc.com

    @compendiumliveinspired
#compendiumliveinspired